MW01559906

THIS BOOK BELONGS TO

Made in the USA
Coppell, TX
28 March 2020

17922731R00066